P.O.W.E.R. Princess Poetry Plus

by Tonja K. Taylor

POWERLight Learning
Fort Worth, Texas

Also by Tonja K. Taylor

POWERLight Lit Tips for Better Teaching
The New Legacy Expanded
P.O.W.E.R. Princess Poetry Plus
The Adventures of Princess Pearl, P.O.W.E.R. Girl!
Your Holy Health: Effective Secrets to Divine Life
Spirit Songs & Stories Enhanced

Watch for more at https://www.faithwriters.com/member-profile.php?id=64826.

Table of Contents

Truly, we are full of power by the Spirit of the LORD. - Micah 3:8

For the kingdom of God consists of *and* is based on not talk but power (moral power and excellence of soul). - I Corinthians 4:20, AMPC

ISBN **978-1-965641-15-6**[3] ebook

ISBN: **978-1-965641-24-8** print

Check out our YouTube channels, "River Rain Creative", and "POWERLight Learning", plus 1,500+ of Tonja's writings on various subjects, at www.FaithWriters.com[4]!

ATOS levels assessed by www.renaissance.com/resources[5]

---

1. http://www.lockman.org/
2. http://www.lockman.org/
3. **https://www.myidentifiers.com/title_registration?isbn=978-1-965641-15-6&icon_type=New**
4. http://www.FaithWriters.com
5. http://www.renaissance.com/resources

Reviews - The Adventures of Princess Pearl, P.O.W.E.R. Girl!

(ATOS 7.92)

Readers from an 8-year-old boy, to a mature woman of 74 and beyond have found **The Adventures of Princess Pearl, *P.O.W.E.R. Girl!*** series to be delightful, insightful, thought-provoking edutainment, that helps engage and empower readers, strengthening literacy, critical thinking, and creativity!

The Adventures of Princess Pearl, *P.O.W.E.R. Girl! I*

"Tonja..it was easy and frankly, a pleasant read—May God richly bless this book—far beyond what you can imagine."—Kim Potter, Founder and Director, A New Thing Ministries, www.anewthingministries.com[1]

"Thank you so much for that wonderful gift. It looks amazing. I'm going to give it to my granddaughter."—Pastor Lynn Hayden, Owner and Director, www.dancingforhim.com[2].

"Tonja... I love it! I can't believe how thorough you are. Your scenes are enticing and you have excellently woven background into the progress of the story..." Abby Kelly, MI, The Predatory Lies of Anorexia: A Survivor's Story

"Princess Pearl is truly a jewel that would be treasured by every young girl...a must have on the bookshelf of anyone striving to training up a child in the way they should go!"—Mallory W., teacher, AR

1. http://www.anewthingministries.com
2. http://www.dancingforhim.com

"Enjoyed reading the book. Loved getting to know Pearl and see how she grows spiritually." —Emily O., former librarian at a Christian school, AR

"You are a good writer and I like that you add the plan of salvation in it. Every pre-teen and teenager should read it!"—Marsha B., 32, Splendora, Texas

"I read the first four chapters and cried... read the book to the girls...they loved it, and they want horses."—Elena N., godmother to four princesses, TX

"It was really good. I will pray. When is the next one going to be ready?"—Alexis, 10, AR

"Thank you for the book. May your book touch many other girls' lives."—Rockell, 13, AR

"My 8-year-old son enjoyed Pearl,"—nurse, 40s, AR

"I read your book and thought it was a great read, especially for preadolescent and adolescent girls and even boys for that matter." –Carol T, 37, social worker, NY

"I really like it. It's a good book. It's funny, Adults like it too. I think it's got a lot of stuff in it that's good for anybody. I want to read it again. Don't let up on your writing!" – M. Rayburn, age 74, Texarkana, AR

"I gave the book to Lexi (granddaughter). She really liked it."—Bonnie B., school secretary, Texarkana, AR

"The books are really special, and the kids would be happy to get them. You are so talented." -Carolyn Spark, (former Coordinator), Operation Christmas Child, Texarkana, AR

The Adventures of Princess Pearl, *P.O.W.E.R. Girl! II:*

"Everything flows well....It was nice to see the relationship between Xi and Pearl develop." - Victoria, 26, AR

"My dear friend your books are very good...GOD is your teacher, what else do you want? Hopefully you can reach many people...with your books, also with your presence talking about our Wonderful GOD and HIS only amazing SON..."—Sara S., 39, grandmother, TX

"It's really amazing how this story spoke to me...Even though it's for children, the lessons taught within are truths that helps adults. I fully recommend people of all ages to read this fun and delightful story!" - Andrew R., 28, biologist, TX

THE ADVENTURES OF PRINCESS Pearl, *P.O.W.E.R. Girl! III:*

"Tonja, you are an amazing writer! I'm so impressed with how you imagined the characters and developed such an awesome storyline to convey the Gospel...Thank you for entrusting me with the chance to read and consider your work!" - Joy W., 56, Teen Counselor &Psychologist, MD

Reviews - Spirit Songs & Stories

(ATOS 7.81)

D*ear Tonja,*

I thought "The Little Lamb and the Special Snowflake" was very well done. You have a gift for writing in a style that is full of beautiful images that will delight children. I also thought the message of the story was very good and very important for children to learn—namely, that what the Lord wants from us is simply...us!....It was to make that possible that He sent Jesus...so that through His perfect sacrifice, we can offer ourselves to God as a "thank offering.".- Bro. Martin Rizley, Magdala, Spain

Dear Tonja, I have just finished reading the story of "The Butterfly and the Mimosa." For me, the message is that God made me special... that I can achieve the purpose of God simply by being me and not trying to be somebody else. As Jesus said, as you did to the least of my brothers so you did unto me. I will take time to be a blessing to someone today.

I like "The King's Horse," because there is a great lesson on realizing the real reason for Jesus's return—to gather people to himself. The story is very creative and really Holy Spirit inspired....After finishing the story, my heart just fell in love with Jesus all the more....l want my life to be the vessel that carries the Lord.

Poems—The poems are centered on biblical characters who we can relate to as human beings. It's gratifying to note that in the lives of believers, God always shows himself strong. He intervenes with power and might.— Regards, Muleba M., Lusaka, Zambia

Dedication

(ATOS 7.55)

To our dear LORD, King Jesus, Who is my life: Thank You for the honor and joy of writing Your words, and may they all be from You!

To my dear husband, church family, other family, and friends, including my faithful reviewers: You're precious to me, and I am so thankful for your love and prayers and help! Truly, anything done for God is a team effort!

To all my dear readers: May this mélange; this mix of songs, psalms, and poems from long ago, through today, be insightful and delightful to you. May you be strengthened, inspired, and motivated to create your own "spirit songs and poems"—in every area of life—to the glory of God!

...12 I am writing to you, little children, because your sins have been forgiven through His name. 13 I am writing to you, fathers, because you know Him who is from the beginning. I am writing to you, young men, because you have overcome the evil one... 14... I have written to you, young men, because you are strong, and the word of God abides in you, and you have overcome the evil one.... - I John 2:12-14, Berean Standard Bible

...A love song. My heart is stirred by a noble as I recite my verses to the king; my tongue is the pen of a skillful writer. – Psalm 45:1, Berean Standard Bible

A Note From Tonja

(ATOS 8.91)

God, Who is a Spirit, lives in our praise; in our worship and adoration of Him. Hallelujah!

[3]**But You are holy, O You Who dwell in [the holy place where] the praises of Israel [are offered].** – Psalm 22:3, AMPC

It is my prayer that this book will inspire you to be free to rejoice and just enjoy praising the LORD—however He leads you to. He loves you and will help you!

Many songs can be structured as poems, and vice versa, although songs can differ in various ways from what we know as poetry, whether it rhymes or not.

You may have sung your own "spirit songs"—simple little melodies that most likely rhymed, when you were happy, or in some place where you felt safe and free.

Spirit songs, as I call them, can also rise up in us—by the Holy Spirit Who is God (Gen. 1:26, AMPC) to strengthen us to overcome challenges in life.

These may or may not rhyme, and are usually deeper, more serious songs of victory, of confidence in the LORD God, the LORD of Hosts that, no matter how life looks at the moment, He is faithful to give us triumph over trouble!

By the way, contrary to what many believe, poetry does *not* have to rhyme! Rhyming poetry usually sounds better to us, and is often called "verse" for greeting cards, jingles for commercials, and many songs.

However, some of the most soul-soothing lyrics go beyond rhyme. For instance, the poetry of the Bible (found mostly in Psalms, at least half of which were written by King David before he became king, does not rhyme. I rest my case. ☺

Let the word of Christ richly dwell within you as you teach and admonish one another with all wisdom, and as you sing psalms, hymns, and spiritual songs with gratitude in your hearts to God. -Colossians 3:16, Berean Standard Bible

The LORD tells us in Colossians 3:16 to minister to Him and to one another in "psalms and hymns and spiritual songs," and these can be as simple as a line or two, to an advanced multi-faceted song requiring many instruments.

Also, Ephesians 5:18-20 (Berean Standard Bible) says: ...**18** Do not get drunk on wine, which leads to reckless indiscretion. Instead, be filled with the Spirit. **19 Speak to one another with psalms, hymns, and spiritual songs. Sing and make music in your hearts to the Lord, 2 0**always giving thanks to God the Father for everything in the name of our Lord Jesus Christ....

God loves your songs to Him—no matter how your voice sounds! He is seeking worshipers in spirit and in truth. The main thing the LORD desires is not for our songs to sound so sweet, as our hearts to echo in the heavens as we pour out our love on Him! Hallelujah!

"God is Spirit, and His worshipers must worship Him in spirit and in truth." – John 4:24, Berean Standard Bible

Who among the 'gods' is like You, O LORD? Who is like You—majestic in holiness, revered with praises, performing wonders?– Exodus 15:11, Berean Standard Bible

How to Write Your Own Tongue Twisters

(ATOS 8.19)

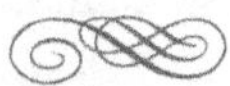

A CHEERFUL HEART IS good medicine, but a broken spirit saps a person's strength. – Prov. 17:22, NLT

Let's activate our creativity by writing tongue twisters! It's easy, fun, and can bring great joy to you, and/or your students—and serve as a catalyst for you to write more and greater things, such as songs and poems. 😊

Here is a piece I did a few years ago, while encouraging some of my elementary online students to work together and enjoy the creative process:

This morning, I wrote a simple sentence as a story starter to help the kids (including English Language Learners) I teach be more creative: "With Sylvia, a bath is *an event*."

After a minute or so, I started expanding upon the idea of "Sylvia," and realized I was writing a tongue twister. I used this to help and delight my students around the world to expand their vocabularies, and otherwise become more fluent in English.

(I also realized I could teach people how to write their own, and have fun being silly and creative, and thus have merry hearts that would bring peace and healing! How good is our God, Elohim the Creator, Who gives us these positive inspirations!)

With the help of the LORD, Who *is* the Author, the Living Word (John 1) this is what I wrote:

Sylvia swan swims successfully as she sings silly songs, so she succeeds in stupefying squids so they will stop swimming and snotting stuff, and swimmers will stop screeching in the streams saying simple shrieks and screams.

I have written many stories and books, and share them with the kids at my church and beyond. So what started as a story prompt ("With Sylvia, a bath is *an event")* birthed a fun tongue twister that could not only help my ELL students, but my American students at church, and more.

(My dear husband suggested I also let them illustrate it. Great idea! So students can illustrate my ideas and theirs. Then it would be their class story.)

The "Sylvia" writing is actually a pretty simple tongue twister (although long) compared to many, but it will suffice (Yes, there's another "S" word for you.).

Now, you can write *your own* tongue twister. It's not that hard. True, some of us like to write more than others and some of us have more experience, but *you can do this!*

Also, you can engage your students and let them "teach" you by giving *you* ideas to write a tongue twister!

Here are steps you can follow to write your own:

1. Pick any noun (which can be a proper noun, like someone's name—but make sure the usage of it is paired with positivity, or at least something really silly that will not bother someone (as much as possible; Romans 12:18) and write it on a white board, your computer, or a piece of paper.

Example: *Carmen*

1. Picture a scenario in your mind and add an action verb or

two, preferably a verb(s) that starts with the same letter as the noun.

Example: Carmen *can't catch*

1. Next add direct objects (which are nouns).

Example: Carmen can't catch *cats*

4. Now add words in proper sentence form, but allow yourself to extend the sentence with as many action verbs, adjectives, adverbs, and nouns as possible using alliteration—using words that start with the same letter.

Example: *Carmen can't catch cats in cages 'cause it's crazily catastrophic and crushes creeds of canine cousins considering creating and cutting contracts.*

1. Tongue twisters rarely make sense, so have fun being nonsensical! Practice saying your tongue twister as quickly and articulately as possible. Enjoy, and make more. This can become a favorite activity, and I believe you will be surprised and delighted at your students' creativity!

Yes, the LORD has done amazing things for us! What joy!
—Psalm 126:3, NLT

Poet's Theorem

©1998 by *Tonja K. Taylor*[1]
(ATOS 8.22)

A JOYFUL HEART IS GOOD medicine, but a broken spirit dries up the bones. – Prov. 17:22, Berean Standard Bible

Most poets and other writers take themselves too seriously.

I have been guilty of such, even for decades.

Now I know, of course, that the LORD is the Author, and I am one of His Royal Scribes.

Let us fix our eyes on Jesus, the author and perfector of our faith, who for the joy set before Him endured the cross, scorning its shame, and sat down at the right hand of the throne of God. – Hebrews 12:2, Berean Standard Bible

I yield to Him, and He makes His words flow through my fingers.

1 Blessed be the LORD, my Rock, who trains my hands for war, my fingers for battle. 2 He is my steadfast love and my fortress, my stronghold and my deliverer. He is my shield, in whom I take refuge, who subdues peoples under me. -Psalm 144:1-2, Berean Standard Bible

I've been writing poetry since I was 9; that makes (literally!) 50 years, or 5 decades! The LORD is a great encourager, and has a great sense of humor. This is what occurred to me one day about my work; my "Poet's Theorem":

---

1. http://www.faithwriters.com/member-profile.php?id=64826

Poet's Theorem

I am a poet.
All poets feel deeply.
Therefore, my poetry is profound.

(copyright 1989 by Tonja K. Taylor, more or less)

According to Google, a theorem is "a general proposition not self-evident but proved by a chain of reasoning; a truth established by means of accepted truths."

So there you have it, my friends. I'm sure you agree! (Right?! But only if you want to. Let the LORD lead you! 😊)

For more proof that my poetry is profound, check out the many songs and poems (and more) on FaithWriters.com!

Speaking of songs and poems, let's get started with the benefits of singing, then help you learn how to write you own songs and poems, or have fun writing even more, even if you've written many.

Remember, *Kaizen*—continuous improvement!

7 Benefits of Singing

(ATOS 7.92)

POEMS CAN BE SONGS, and vice versa, with a few differences here and there. Regardless of the form, the LORD your Daddy God loves it when you sing to Him, and He's NOT judging how you sound. He is listening to your heart of love for Him! Hallelujah!—note from Tonja

1 O sing to the Lord a new song; sing to the Lord, all the earth! 2 Sing to the Lord, bless (affectionately praise) His name; show forth His salvation from day to day. 3 Declare His glory among the nations, His marvelous works among all the peoples. 4 For great is the Lord and greatly to be praised; He is to be reverently feared and worshiped above all [so-called] gods.—Psalm 96:1-4, AMPC

When I did a topic search for "sing" just now in the Amplified Classic Bible (AMPC) online, there were 234 Scriptures talking about singing!

God loves singing, and it is said by some Hebrew scholars that the LORD God *sang* the earth into existence!

Truly, God is *the coolest!* (Over 20 years ago, I was working an evangelistic outreach in another city, and I was overwhelmed with thankfulness and joy to be a part of God's work in the earth. I looked up and said out loud, "God, You are so cool!" "The coolest!" He replied quickly, in my heart! Amen and amen!)

GOD—Elohim, the Creator and Sustainer of the Heavens and the earth—is the "last Frontier," and the more we explore of Him, the Majesty, the more we realize the truly awesome endlessness of the living God, Jesus Christ the King! He truly is The Awesome God! (Psalm 68:37)

Who is like You, O Lord, among the gods? Who is like You, glorious in holiness, awesome in splendor, doing wonders? – Exodus 15:11, AMPC

Now, where was I? Oh yes, talking about singing. Just focusing for a bit on the awesome (I only use that word for Him, for there is nothing (to me) deserving of that word other than the LORD our God and His work!) goodness of God (and everything in our lives that's good is from God!

Let them confess and praise Your great name, awesome and reverence inspiring! It is holy, and holy is He! – Psalm 99:3, AMPC

When we are little, singing often spontaneously occurs.

As older teens and adults, we still like to sing along to songs we love, but our singing is usually much less spontaneous. However, when we are full of God, we often cannot help but thank Him by singing His praise—and there are *many* benefits to that!

<u>1. One is just sheer joy—gladness!</u> We just delight in how good God has been to us, to love and save and protect and direct and provide and teach us, and be with us always.

<u>2. Another is replacing the wicked</u> (depressing, frustrating, irritating, tormenting, etc.<u>) thoughts with the righteous</u> <u>thoughts</u> (love, peace, joy, thankfulness, righteousness-conscious; God-with-us-and-for-us conscious, victory, abundance, freedom, favor, healing, strength, restoration, etc.).

<u>3. An additional benefit can be deliverance and healing occurring in ourselves and others, as the Holy Spirit leads</u>—for when we sing praises to the LORD, the enemy is ashamed and defeated (reminded of his defeat at the cross!) and cannot stand to stay, and the LORD Jesus

Christ is magnified and can do great and mighty things, for He lives in our praise!

4. A powerful one is to bring praise and glory and honor to the LORD, Who is worthy of all our worship!

5. One of the best (and they're all good benefits!) is that singing to the LORD can grow your faith, for when we sing praises to the LORD, we become more aware of how much more loving, faithful, powerful, and gracious He is!

6. Another could be that others are liberated to be free to sing to the LORD, when your kids or more hear you sing.

7. You can receive divine direction as you worship the LORD in song! God's Presence is in true worship!

As one preacher stated, with a chuckle, "We can all sing, but we should not all record."

If you don't think your voice sounds good enough for recording, no worries. You can get training to help with that, if you want to perform a lot in public or record, or both.

Here's the best part: When we sing from our hearts to our dear Daddy God, He loves it! It brings Him joy, and that is the best benefit of all! Just like we love it when our little ones sing, how much more does our Daddy God Who created us in love and gives us every breath, loves our songs—in tune or not?! Hallelujah!

How great and gracious is our God, so, let us **6 Sing praises to God, sing praises! Sing praises to our King, sing praises!** 7 **For God is the King of all the earth; sing praises in a skillful psalm and with understanding.—Psalm 47:6-7, AMPC**

Amen and amen!

6 Reasons to Praise the LORD!

(ATOS 6.56)

JESUS THE ONLY SAVIOR of the world, and the LORD of all, is so worthy of our praise and worship! When we focus on Him, He is glorified, and we can forget challenges, and realize and rejoice that He is so much bigger than them all—and for and with us always! Hallelujah! (note from Tonja)

(Note from Tonja:) The LORD commands us to praise and worship Him but it is for US, not Him!

Let the word [spoken by] Christ (the Messiah) have its home [in your hearts and minds] and dwell in you in [all its] richness, as you teach and admonish and train one another in all insight and intelligence and wisdom [in spiritual things, and as you sing] psalms and hymns and spiritual songs, making melody to God with [His] grace in your hearts. – Col. 3:16, AMPC

1. *He is worthy*! John 1, 3:16, Genesis, Heb 13:8!
2. It changes us—heals, delivers, teaches, frees, restores; we become more like Him!
3. It amplifies our awareness of Him and His goodness, His power, His mercy, His grace, His faithfulness, and more!
4. It amplifies/builds our faith!
5. It helps us forget ourselves and others and focus totally on the

positive—HIM!!

6. It is one of the most powerful ways to say, "THANK YOU!"

JESUS IS LORD!

Introduction to Song/Poem Writing

(ATOS 6.92 for article + songs/poems)

6 **Let everything that has breath and every breath of life praise the Lord! Praise the Lord! (Hallelujah!)** – Psalm 150:6, AMPC

You are never too young to write a song/psalm or poem, especially for God! He loves it when you write for Him!

As God says in His Word: "Let no one despise or think less of you because of your youth, but be an example (pattern) for the believers in speech, in conduct, in love, in faith, and in purity." – I Tim. 4:12, AMPC

He will help you to write neat stuff that helps you and other people know He loves them and wants them to have a great life!

(Here's a secret: *God* is actually the *real* Writer, through His Spirit! 😊 He is the Creator of all things good, and He will help you; He will flow through you with His creative Self, so you'll actually be writing things together—like He's flowing through me right now, to create this book! COOL, huh?!)

There are many ways you can write a song/psalm, or a poem, and sometimes, they are easily interchangeable; that is, the same structure can be either a poem or a song.

(However, official "songs" as we know them today often have several distinct parts. In addition to the verses, they usually have at least some of these: intro, pre-chorus, chorus, a bridge, and an outro. But that's another writing.)

Our minds really like it when poems and songs have regular rhythm and rhyme, such as the sing-song verse writings in greeting cards, and/or jingles, or tunes, that we hear on commercials.

Often, these are easy to memorize, and it is good in many ways to write simple lyrics, so we can learn and memorize songs quickly; so that they are easy to get them in our hearts—where they can help us keep our minds on God and the good things He gives us.

As He commands us to do in Colossians 3:2 (Berean Standard Bible): **"Set your minds on things above, not on earthly things."**

(However, of course, if we learn and memorize negative chants/words/songs, then of course, then those not-good words will cause negative thoughts, and from our thoughts come our decisions, and our decisions cause our actions and words—which shape our lives.

So, we ask the LORD to give us wisdom and to help us "choose life" (to choose good; Deut. 30:19; John 10:10)!

Really, then, we can take any subject and, with the LORD's help, and with a thesaurus and/or a rhyming dictionary, we can create a short, meaningful rhyming song that we can memorize quickly, and even teach to others.

One example that many of us know is "Jesus Loves Me", (John 3:16; John 15:12-13; Romans 5:8; I John 4:16;)), which was very easy for us to learn and put in our hearts, to sing with others and ourselves.

(Even adults need to sing to Him, for we are all children of God when we have asked His Son, King Jesus, to forgive and cleanse us of our sins, and be our Savior and LORD! John 3:14-17, and Romans 5:6 and 10:13!).

The first part of the song (now in public domain) says: *"Jesus s me, this I know, for the Bible tells me so. Little ones to Him belong; they are weak, but He is strong."*

So, although there are not many words, there is a lot of meaning! It has regular rhyme and rhythm, which is very pleasing to our minds—and the message is the best, for it is the Truth of the Word: *GOD LOVES US*. Hallelujah!

Here's another example of a "simple song/poem" that is full of positivity! It was created years ago, by dear students in one of my many online classes.

We started with them sharing ideas for the They chose to create a song/poem that bragged on their parents, which was very pleasing to me—and to God!

As they shared things about their parents' love for them, I wrote their ideas on the computer whiteboard for the whole class to see at once.

I listened to their ideas of how to complete the lines and phrases, and how to switch them around, till the whole class (5 students, from what I remember) was satisfied with the song/poem.

(My students chose to write their song/poem in first person point of view, thus the "I" of the narrator/singer/poet.)

The song/poem they created has a nice three-beats-per-line rhythm, and the lines are in couplets (two lines per unit, or section).

After I finished typing it for them, one boy came up with a melody for it, from what I remember.

I was impressed with their work, and told them I was going to publish it as I bragged on them!

So here you go. (Enjoy, and may this inspire you to go for it, and start creating your own song/poems of positivity!)

The Good-Parent Rap

by Mrs. Taylor's JWC Fourth-Grade Class:

My folks are super-heroes
They love me lots and lots

They take me shopping, buy me stuff
From since I was a tot

They help me when I need it;
How to live right every way

Faithfully, they teach me—
They help me every day.

They play many games with me
And teach me to be free

They really care about me—
They are my family!

Wasn't that great?! You can do the same thing—with yourself and God, or you and friends, or yourself and family, etc. (God will *always* be part of any positive creativity in any form, even if you aren't aware of Him. He loves you and is with you always!)

In the beginning was the Word, and the Word was with God, and the Word was God. He was with God in the beginning. Through Him all things were made, and without Him nothing was made that has been made. – John 1:1-3, Berean Standard Bible

Behold what manner of love the Father has given to us, that we should be called the children of God. And that is what we are! The reason the world does not know us is that is did not know Him. – I John 3:1, Berean Standard Bible

Another example of creating a "simple" song from Scripture is to take one verse and repeat it. After all, as I used to tease my dear daughter, when I homeschooled her in her 6th and 7th grade years (about 15 years ago, at the time of this writing), "Repetition's how we learn. Repetition's how we learn. Repetition's how..." 😊.

So, *sing, sing, sing,* and the more you sing the right, good things, the better you will feel!

Even more exciting than that is this: When we praise the LORD; even when we're singing positive things that aren't openly about Him,

He likes it (for all positive things truly come from and through Him!)—and He draws near!

...for in Him we live and move and have our being, as also some of your own poets have said, 'For we are also His offspring.' – Acts 17:28, AMPC

16 **For it was in Him that all things were created, in heaven and on earth, things seen and things unseen, whether thrones, dominions, rulers, or authorities; all things were created *and* exist through Him [by His service, intervention] and in *and* for Him.** – Colossians 1:16, AMPC

When the LORD God of Heaven and earth draws near; makes Himself known; when we experience Him (which is what "manifested" means)—then we are helped and convicted and comforted and strengthened and encouraged and enlightened and enraptured and directed!

We are changed in good ways, because we understand more of how He, the Great I AM, loves us so much! Hallelujah!

And all of us, as with unveiled face, [because we] continued to behold [in the Word of God] as in a mirror the glory of the Lord, are constantly being transfigured into His very own image in ever increasing splendor and from one degree of glory to another; [for this comes] from the Lord [Who is] the Spirit. – 2 Cor. 3:18, AMPC

So, the LORD showed me over 20 years ago how to create a very simple but fun "spirit song" (psalm) or poem from Psalm 126:3 (which is the theme verse for my marriage, and we'll be married 20 years Oct. 1!).

Also, this is not really *my* song; these are God's words in the Bible, from Psalm 126:3!

The LORD has done great things for us,
And we are filled with joy!
The LORD has done great things for us,
And we are filled with joy!

Joy! Joy! We are filled with joy!
The LORD has done great things for us,
And we are filled with joy!
(Psalm 126:3, Berean Standard Bible)

This song (which is also a Psalm) repeats the Scripture several times (which is an excellent and fun way to learn and get Bible verses into our hearts!), and has a regular rhythm. We could clap our hands as we sing it, and bring the LORD and each other even more joy. 😊

So YOU can do the same thing! Pray. Ask the LORD to show you a Scripture that you can easily convert to a poem/psalm/spirit song. He will!

Write it down or enter it on your device. Record it with your voice (Remember, He just asks us to "make a joyful noise"—not to sing like the super-stars! He loves to hear you praise and worship Him, and your voice doing that always sounds lovely to Him!).

4 Make a joyful noise to the LORD, all the earth; break forth—let your cry ring out, and sing praises! Psalm 98:4, Berean Standard Bible

If you play an instrument, you could also ask the LORD to help you pick out the melody, to go with the Scripture and any other lyrics/ words He gives you for the song.

Relax, ask the Holy Spirit to teach you (for He is the Master Teacher Who leads us into better and higher and greater things, for our best and joy, and His glory and joy!

26 But the Advocate, the Holy Spirit, whom the Father will send in My name, will teach you all things and will remind you of everything I have told you.– John 14:26, Berean Standard Bible

You can do this, and you'll get it, and then, the LORD can use your "simple spirit-song" to help you and other people in wonderful ways! He will also multiply your efforts, and can, like He has me, give you many, many more spirit-songs (2 Cor. 9:10, Eph. 3:20)! You may even get to teach others how to do this really cool thing of creating songs of positivity, if you want to. 😊

Then there are the songs/psalms and poems that don't rhyme (Yes, contrary to what my husband and some others like to believe, true poetry does *not* have to rhyme! 😊),

and this is best for certain works, which would not have the same depth if they did.

Poems and songs that don't rhyme are usually, (not always) slower, and connote a deeper thoughtfulness; as if the poet or psalmist is pondering the most important things of life.

Here is a short teaching on this subject: https://www.youtube.com/watch?v=74zsaHsE5oQ

The Psalms in the Bible are to me, very beautiful, containing every emotion a human can feel—and none of them rhyme (in English, anyway, as far as I can tell). Yet they have rhythm and structure. Here is an example:

1[1] Rejoice in the LORD, O righteous ones; it is fitting for the upright to praise Him. 2[2] Praise the LORD with the harp; make music to Him with ten strings. 3[3] Sing to Him a new song; play skillfully with a shout of joy. – Psalm 148:1-3, Berean Standard Bible

Since we're talking about non-rhyming songs and poetry now, let's look at my poem, "Choices," originally written in 1992:

Choices

© 1992 by Tonja K. Taylor

I hear the lovely mourning doves...
Are they lamenting my past choices?

How do I choose to spend
Each golden hour of my life?

---

1. https://biblehub.com/psalms/33-1.htm
2. https://biblehub.com/psalms/33-2.htm
3. https://biblehub.com/psalms/33-3.htm

Is it worry about things
And working through pain,

Or letting go and letting God—
The Maker of all things—

Compose the notes of every day
Into a song of truth
that gives me wings?

I decide to trust Him!

Then there are some poems and songs that have slight rhyme, or "off rhyme", which means the rhyme is close enough in the vowel sounds and/or the last syllable to make them qualify for "rhyme."

"A Lake of Light," that I wrote about 5 years ago, is an example of such a poem that has some "off" or "close" rhymes (lithe, light, white, bright, life; the sound of the long "I" in the middle of those words echoes through the poem. Also, the long "A" in spray and lake echo.):

A Lake of Light

© May 19, 2020 by Tonja K. Taylor

A soft sweet shade
The breeze in my hair
The light on the lake
Fountain soft and lithe
a spray of light
a spray of white
The waving wind—
bright water dancing
Ducks glide on glass
teeming with life

a lake of light
a lake of life

ONCE MORE JESUS ADDRESSED the crowd. He said, I am the Light of the world. He who follows Me will not be walking in the dark, but will have the Light which is Life. - John 8:12, (AMPC)

It is wonderful, and very powerful, when the LORD by His Holy Spirit (Whom many Hebrew scholars believe *sang* the world into existence!) gives us beautiful words!

Here is one method to get you started writing a song or poem (and you can also use this to brainstorm ideas for a paper or book you may want to write, or even to help you make a decision about something):

1. Think of a subject you want to write about.
2. Draw a circle in the middle of the paper or on your device.
3. Write/draw that subject, like "My Pet" in the middle of the circle.
4. Draw lots of lines from the outside of the circle to various points on the paper/screen.
5. Write a word or short phrase and/or draw a picture of what you want to say about the subject in the middle of the circle, for instance, "sweet", "furry", "playful", "loves to fetch", "is my reading buddy", "listens to me sing", "loves me", "walks with me", and so on—anything you can think of about your subject, that you want to put in the poem or song.
6. Now take those words and phrases, and start putting them in order, rearranging as you like; rather like more of a Rubics cube than a picture puzzle. (After all, it is your work, and only you will know when it is right; when your soul is satisfied!)
7. Sometimes you may need to work on your song/poem for a while, then ignore it for a while; a few hours, a day, a week, or longer. Your subconscious (which is always awake, even when

your body sleeps, and which the Holy Spirit Who is one with the Creator, Elohim, works with in your life) will continue to work on it—so you may awaken in the middle of the night with the perfect addition or ending!

   a. Sometimes, it takes a while for your lovely jewel to be completely polished; to fully shine in all its facets. So, no worries! You can start a new song/poem, or three, or ten—and come back to the first one, when the creative flow leads you to do so! (Note: Actually, Elohim the Creator is always awake and ready to create, for He never grows tired nor weary, nor does He sleep or slumber (Psalm 121:4)!

8. If you don't feel like you can go further, you can ask the LORD, the Holy Spirit, Elohim (He has many names, but He is one God (I Tim. 2:5)), to inspire you more, and He will. It may not come immediately, but He will help you!
9. When you are pleased with your work, read it out loud first to yourself, to see how it sounds to your ear. Sometimes, what we read on the page does not sound the same when we read it out loud. You want your song/poem to satisfy you when you hear it. You can also have a friend or family member read your work out loud, so you can hear how it sounds through them. Be open to suggestions, because they may have some, and that may help you. Besides, you can always have more than one version of your work; the one you like just the way you write it, and another, with some changes that friends or family may give you. 😊
10. Record it into your device, so you'll have a keepsake, and can, with your parent's or teacher's permission, upload it to share with others!

The rest of the book has many song/poems, that I've written through the years. These are not all, for I don't have some of them I wrote years ago, but I believe this book has enough to truly motivate you that, if I can do it, *so can you!*

Here's another, which I wrote to my dear mother years ago, to inspire you to be more thankful for your good parents!

Thank You, Dear Mama,
For teaching me
To sew, to mow, to grow—
Fruits and veggies, and my mind;
To give and work hard; to be kind.
To follow my dreams, to know that life
Is more than it seems; to forsake strife;
To love our God and all others—
You're one of the best mothers!
I love you and am so thankful for you!
© December 2019, by Tonja K. Taylor

No matter your age, *you can do this!* I was making up songs and singing them to God when I was 5, for I remember it vividly, especially as I was "in motion"—swinging. 😊

Following are a few more of my songs.

https://www.youtube.com/watch?v=Qj_s3JC7WEM

All of This and Chocolate Too!

(ATOS 6.40 note + poem/song)

NOTE FROM TONJA: THE LORD loves you and will give you many wonderful spirit-songs as you yield to Him and work with Him. (SO GO FOR IT!) The more of His Word you have in you, the more you know His love for you, the more you can do Ephesians 5:19:

19 Speak out to one another in psalms and hymns and spiritual songs, offering praise with voices [[a[1]]and instruments] and making melody with all your heart to the Lord, 20 At all times and for everything giving thanks in the name of our Lord Jesus Christ to God the Father. - Eph. 5:19-20, AMPC

One day, years ago, I was (really) thinking about my wonderful life in Christ, and also the organic chocolate malted milk balls that my husband and I had bought the day before. I was anticipating eating one, and the Holy Spirit suddenly gave me this song, called "All This and Chocolate Too!"

The LORD is good
to me and you
The LORD is good
that's always true
And there's nothing we

---

1. **https://www.biblegateway.com/ passage/?search=eph%205%3A19-20&version=AMPC#fen-AMPC-29322a**

could ever do
To make Him stop loving
me and you
He gives us all things
to enjoy
Like hills and streams
and birds of blue
And friends and church
and then Himself—
All of this
and chocolate too!
Here's what I know is true:
all this and chocolate too!
I know what the LORD is gonna do—
those mighty things, for me and you
He takes the old
and makes us new
He helps us learn to eschew
the bad, the yuck, the evil too
I know what the LORD is gonna do—
just what He said, for He is ever true.
Here's what I know for me and you—
all of this and chocolate too!

So this is an excellent example of a poem that is also a song. It is both!

I sing it happily, with a fast and confident voice, for the LORD is so good, and it reminds me of Psalm 34:8: **O taste and see that the Lord [our God] is good! Blessed (happy, fortunate, to be envied) is the man who trusts *and* takes refuge in Him.**

Go for it. *You can do this!*

Jesus Did It and I Believe It!

© 7/27/22 by Tonja K. Taylor
(ATOS 3.69)

(WITH A SWINGY, LIGHT-hearted, confident, and victorious voice—and more so every time you sing it!)

I have told you these things so that in Me you may have peace. In the world you will have tribulation. But take courage; I have overcome the world!—John 16:33, Berean Study Bible

Jesus did it, and I believe it—
That is my true story!

Jesus did it, and I receive it—
I give Him all the glory!

Jesus did it, and I believe it!
Jesus did it, and I receive it!
Jesus did it, and I perceive it—

Glory Hallelu!

He always does
what He says He'll do!
Forever He is good and true!

Hallelujah, Hallelu!

Yes amen!

Jesus said it, and I believe it—
This is my true story!

Jesus said it, and I receive it—
I give Him all the glory!

Jesus did it, and I believe it!
Jesus did it, and I receive it!
Jesus did it, and I perceive it—
Glory Hallelu!

He always does
what He says He'll do!

Forever He is good and true!
Hallelujah, Hallelu!
Hallelujah, Hallelu!

Yes, amen!

(repeat as desired!)

But thanks be to God, Who in Christ always leads us in triumph [as trophies of Christ's victory] and through us spreads and makes evident the fragrance of the knowledge of God everywhere,--2 Corinthians 2:14, AMPC

The P.O.W.E.R. Princess

(from *P.O.W.E.R. Girl Adventures* books)
© 2020 by Tonja K. Taylor
(ATOS 9.00 - intro + poem)

4 My message sand and my preaching were not with persuasive words of wisdom, but with a demonstration of the Spirit's power, 5 so that your faith would not rest on men's wisdom, but on God's power….- I Cor. 2:4, Berean Standard Bible

[4]**But to those who are called, whether Jew or Greek (Gentile), Christ [is] the Power of God and the Wisdom of God.** – I Corinthians 1:24, AMPC

[20]**For the kingdom of God consists of *and* is based on not talk but power (moral power and excellence of soul).** – I Corinthians 4:20, AMPC

Princess Pearl (The heroine of the *P.O.W.E.R. Girl Adventures* series) is a Princess of *P.O.W.E.R.*: *Purposeful Operations With Eternal Rewards.*

She has a P.O.W.E.R. Rock. It speaks to her (The "P.O.W.E.R. Rock" is The WORD of God—JESUS, Who is Yahweh Tsuri, the Rock!). She listens to, sings, and writes P.O.W.E.R. Songs, and she has a P.O.W.E.R. Sword—Her mouth!

Following is "The P.O.W.E.R. Princess" poem!

The P.O.W.E.R. Princess Poem

(ATOS 4.0)

When darkness approaches
She knows how to fight
For she is full of
The P.O.W.E.R. of Light
She understands
She has already won
For she is clothed
With the strength of the Son—
The Spirit of God
With Whom she is one
He enlightens her on
How things are done
With His Spirit-wind
She learns to run
And she's satisfied
With amazing fun!

P.O.W.E.R. Princess Affirmations

© 2018 by Tonja K. Taylor
(ATOS 6.25)

THE LORD GAVE ME THESE Word-based affirmations when I taught fourth grade in a small rural public school. The kids loved it, and competed with each other to lead the class in these affirmations every morning, even when the whiteboard would not work, because they had hidden these positive life-changing declarations in their hearts! Hallelujah!

Using my power of choice,
I control myself.
I show respect to myself and others.
I am wise, so I obey.
I am excellent.
I am trustworthy.
I am quick to help others.
I am special and loved, and I believe it.

You can choose to say them daily! Because they are all based on the Word of God, these words when spoken can definitely wash and renew your mind from wrong thinking, to help train it to be full of *the power of positivity,* and to help you and your loved one(s) make right choices! God is a *positive* God.

(The LORD said) **"Today I have given you the choice between life and death, between blessings and curses. Now I call on heaven and earth to witness the choice you make. Oh, that you would choose life, so that you and your descendants might live!"**— Duet. 30:19, NLT

The Princess Pearl Poem

Tonja K. Taylor, ©2021
(ATOS 6.30)

Princess Pearl is quite a girl,
A royal delight.
Her Kingdom banner does unfurl;
A flowing flag of Light.
With a crown she can't see
And a heart full of glee,
With a lovely white robe
From her Father God's globe,
With a lilt and a twirl,
In a sparkling swirl,
In the power of His might,
She shines Jesus' light;
She likes horses and flowers,
Flowing water springs,
Music from flutes
And from old harps with strings;
Trail rides and sunsets,
Rainbows and stars,
Bluebirds and cake,
And sweet chocolate bars.
She writes songs to God,

Many poems for Him,
While up in her treehouse
Till daylight grows dim.
She solves mysteries,
Rewrites histories
Of people—once sad—
That her love has made glad.
She blesses and gives
And joyfully lives
Always, every day
Helping those on her way;
To teach them to love,
To revere God above,
To give Him their best,
And find peace and rest;
To know that King Jesus
Is coming so soon;
To honor and worship Him—
To give Him heart-room!

AS FOR ME, HOWEVER, I am filled with power by the Spirit of the LORD, with justice and courage...– Micah 3:8, Berean Standard Bible

For the kingdom of God is not a matter of talk but of power. – I Corinthians 4:20, Berean Standard Bible

Water is a Living Thing

(ATOS 7.07)

Water is a living thing
A necessary brook or spring
To cleanse
To nourish
To bring new life
Ever moving
Ever giving
All its fountains lithe and living
Smooth as glass or capped with white
We're drawn to its refreshing sight
Peaceful as a zephyr breeze
Bringing souls to bended knees
To pray when raging in the storm
Sculpting mountains into form
Cleansing beaches
Changing lands
Washing humanity's soiled hands
Thrilling seekers with a fountain
Drop by drop
Eroding mountain

Nourishing a dying man
Oasis in a sun-scorched land

Delighting swimmers
Cruisers too
Needed more than daily food
Wars of wells vital to life
Habitat of many creatures
Full of ever-changing features
Symbol of a brand-new life
Cleansing wounds made from strife
Flowing free to wash and give
New strength for weak ones now to live
Water is a living thing
An ever-flowing mountain stream
That represents the Holy One
Who walked upon the sea and won!

He who believes in Me [who cleaves to *and* trusts in *and* relies on Me] as the Scripture has said, From his innermost being shall flow [continuously] springs and rivers of living water. – John 7:38, AMPC

You Are the Son

© by Tonja K. Taylor
(ATOS 6.38)

AND SIMON PETER ANSWERED and said, Thou art the Christ, the Son of the living God. And Jesus answered and said unto him, Blessed art thou, Simon Barjona, for flesh and blood hath not revealed it unto thee, but my Father, which is in heaven.—Matthew 16:16-17, KJV

You are the Son
You are the Word
You are the One

You are the Son
You are the Word
And You have won

(CHORUS):
You are the Word and You are the Son
You are the true and living One
You are the One that leads me to
The Word—to You, the Son

You are the Word with Whom I'm One

I'm in You
And the Spirit too
Spirit and Word and I are one
In YOU.........

You are the Revelation
You are supreme sensation
You are the invitation
To be free of sin and strife

You are the Answer
The holy, divine Dancer
Who romances us through life...

You are the Word and You are the Son
You are the true and living One
You are the One that leads me to
The Word—to You, the Son

You are the Word with Whom I'm One

You are the Son
You are the Word
You are the One

You are the Son
You are the Word
And You have won!

JESUS IS LORD!

...4 So He became as far superior to the angels as the name He has inherited is excellent beyond theirs. 5 For the which of the angels did God ever say: "You are My Son; today I have become

Your Father"? or again: "I will be His Father, and He will be My Son"? 6 And again, when God brings His firstborn into the world, He says: "Let all God's angels worship Him."...- Hebrews 1:4-6, Berean Standard Bible

My God Loves Me

©2011 by Tonja K. Taylor
(ATOS 4.0)
(Fast, victorious! Sing all caps words louder)

MY GOD LOVES ME,
And I
TRUST HIM totally,
'Cause He
DIED on the CROSS for me,
And SET ME FREE!
My God LOVES me,
And I
TRUST HIM totally,
'Cause He
DIED on the CROSS for me,
And LIVES now
InSIDE me!
(repeat as you wish!)

He put a new song in my mouth, a hymn of praise to our God. Many will see and fear (revere and worship) and put their trust and confident reliance in the LORD. – Psalm 40:3 (AMPC)

A Big Family

© 2020 by Tonja Taylor[1]
(ATOS 6.0)

14... FOR THIS REASON I bow my knees before the Father, 15
from whom every family in heaven and on earth derives its name. 16
I ask that out of the riches of His glory He may strengthen you with
power through His Spirit in your inner being... - Ephesians 3:14-16,
Berean Standard Bible

Thank You for Your mercy, Jesus,
Thank You for Your grace.
Thank You for coming to earth
To show Your loving face.

Thank You for Your awesomeness
That lets all people see
That You came to sacrifice Yourself
To have a great big Family!

Thank You that You've chosen us
With great delight and glee
To be Your precious Children—
Part of Your Royal Family!

1. http://www.faithwriters.com/member-profile.php?id=64826

A Commercial for Summer

© 1979, slightly revised 2020 by Tonja K. Taylor[1]
(ATOS 6.91)

...AND BE NOT GRIEVED and depressed, for the joy of the Lord is your strength and stronghold. – Neh. 8:10, AMPC

Summer is the time
To take a dip in the pool,
To go on picnics
And dress light to keep cool.

School has let out,
So you are free
To wade in the pool
Or climb a tree,

To have a race,
Or a party
To spend more time
With your family,

To fish or swim
Or water ski.
Enjoy it now—

1. http://www.faithwriters.com/member-profile.php?id=64826

Do enjoy being free!

I'm Rock Solid

©2009 by Tonja K. Taylor
(ATOS 12.0)

"Trust confidently in the LORD forever [He is your fortress, your shield, your banner], For the LORD God is an everlasting Rock [the Rock of Ages.]" – Isaiah 26:4, AMP

(Pop beat, happy)
I'm rock solid
I'm rock solid
I'm a living stone
I'm rock solid
I'm rock solid
But not on my own
I'm being built into a temple
A temple of His praise
Together with other
Covenant kids
I'll praise Him all my days
I'm rock solid
I'm rock solid
I'm a living stone

I'm rock solid
I'm rock solid
But not on my own
Living stone by living stone
Together we will be
Worshiping the El Shaddai
The LORD our Rock
Most High
I'm rock solid
I'm rock solid
I'm a living stone
I'm rock solid
I'm rock solid
But not on my own
Together with other
Covenant kids
Together we will be
The mighty Church of Jesus
Full and healed and free!

As the Eagle Goes

(ATOS 8.21)

The eagle is a bird of noble birth,
Sober and majestic, full of grace;
Meant to soar above the winds of earth,
And focus on the sun's eternal face.
The eagle's born into a downy nest,
But as he grows, he feels the thorny stings;
And forced to leave the safety of his rest,
He falls and learns to use his gift of wings.
The eagle doesn't struggle with his foe;
He takes the serpent in his taloned lock
And skimming clouds, he drops it far below,
Where it will meet destruction at the rock.
The eagle when he's ill complains to none
But lies upon the rock that's bathed in light,
Welcoming the healing of the sun—
Or soaring in his spirit's final flight.
The eagle doesn't struggle with the wind;
He simply bides his time and when it's right,
He lifts his wings and feels himself ascend,
And glories in the freedom of his flight.

Pity for the Angels

(ATOS 8.31)

Mighty messengers of God,
Supernatural bearers of the Sword;
Winged warriors in white,
Protecting me from serpent and from stone
Basking in eternal Light,
They look upon God's face and sing His praise;
But still, I pity them—
For they can never know Salvation's joy.

…4 SO HE BECAME AS FAR superior to the angels as the name He has inherited is excellent beyond theirs. 5 For the which of the angels did God ever say: "You are My Son; today I have become Your Father"? or again: "I will be His Father, and He will be My Son"? 6 And again, when God brings His firstborn into the world, He says: "Let all God's angels worship Him."…- Hebrews 1:4-6, Berean Standard Bible

Ambitions

© 1994, slight update 2023 by *Tonja K. Taylor*[1]
(ATOS 5.95)

Take my yoke upon you. Let me teach you, because I am humble and gentle at heart, and you will find rest for your souls. For my yoke is easy to bear, and the burden I give you is light.—Matthew 11:29-30, NLT

I'll live the wild adventures
That lie waiting on my shelves,
I'll find the hidden strengths
We all search for in ourselves.
I'll relax a little bit
About my salt, sugar intake
I'll not count the non-important
Daily errors that I make.
I'll be kinder to my neighbor,
Helpful to my fellow man,
I'll visit friends and loved ones
Not just "one day when I can".
I'll see the sunshine through the rain
Cherish the good, throw out the bad,
And remember to be thankful
For the blessed life I've had.

1. *http://www.faithwriters.com/member-profile.php?id=64826*

Has Anyone Seen My Aplomb?

(ATOS 8.89)

Has anyone seen it—my dear aplomb?
Maybe I left it behind at home;
Or put it on a secret shelf,
To wear when I didn't like myself.
I had it yesterday; it was clearly seen,
Or so to my keen intellect it seemed;
Didn't I infer what they implied?
I thought 'twas my aplomb they spied,
Sparkling, striking, powerfully pleasing;
"It becomes you," they said—
Then again, it might have been
That they were only teasing.
Surely it didn't fall and slip
Down the sink while I did dishes—
Now lost on some iridescent trip
Of ethereal suds and wishes?
Did the maid, in cleaning determination
Think it dust or an aberration,
And remove it forever from its place
In the room where I put on my face?
I wore it with charm and poise, and grace.

With style, panache, finesse,
But now I've misplaced my dear aplomb
And everything's a mess.
It's quite the *faux pas* I have made
I guess; Alas! But even so,
The *moi* I was I wouldn't trade
For the new me I now know.

WHAT TIME I AM AFRAID, I will have confidence in and put my trust and reliance in You. – Psalm 56:3, AMPC

For You are my hope; O Lord God, You are my trust from my youth and the source of my confidence. – Psalm 71:5, AMPC

I have told you these things, so that in Me you may have [perfect] peace and confidence. In the world you have tribulation and trials and distress and frustration; but be of good cheer [take courage; be confident, certain, undaunted]! For I have overcome the world. [I have deprived it of power to harm you and have conquered it for you.] – John 16:33, AMPC

(Underline emphasis mine. Let our confidence; poise; "coolness"; etc, flow from our belief that GOD loves us!)

Great Things

(ATOS 3.86)

**1 When the Lord brought back the captives [who returned] to
Zion, we were like those who dream [it seemed so unreal]. [2]Then
were our mouths filled with laughter, and our tongues with singing.
Then they said among the nations, The Lord has done great things
for them. [3]The Lord has done great things for us! We are glad! –**
Psalm 126:1-3, AMPC

(Upbeat with joy and thanksgiving; sing words in ALL CAPS louder)

The LORD has done great things for us,
And we are filled with joy!
The LORD has done great things for us,
And we are filled with joy!
JOY! JOY! We are filled with JOY!
The LORD has done great things for us,
And WE ARE FILLED WITH JOY!
The LORD has done great things for us,
And He will do much more!

The LORD has done great things for us,

And He will do much more!
MORE! MORE! He will do MUCH MORE!
The LORD has done GREAT THINGS FOR US!
And HE WILL DO MUCH MORE!

Jesus, My Friend

©2010 by Tonja K. Taylor
(ATOS 6.7)

AND THE SCRIPTURE WAS fulfilled that says, "Abraham believed God, and it was credited to him as righteousness," and he was called God's friend. - James 2:23 NIV

(Slow, loving, worshipful style)
JESUS my Friend
I love You
JESUS my Friend
I love You!
Not all my friends are always friends
But there is One I trust
Who always loves and helps me
You see He really must
Because He made a Promise
For eternity to me
That wherever I am,
He will always be
JESUS my Friend
I love You
JESUS my Friend

I love You!

He has healed all my diseases and
Forgiven all my sins
When I feel discouraged
He reminds me that I win
He's returning very soon
And I'll see His holy grin—
He's so wonderful I want to
Sing to Him again
JESUS my Friend
I love You
JESUS my Friend
I love You!

It Just Gets Better

©2008 by Tonja K. Taylor
(ATOS 3.63)

We obey and serve and spend our days in prosperity and our years in pleasures. - Job 36:11 NIV

(THE LORD GAVE ME THIS when my daughter was little (about 25 years ago!), and as a single divorced mom, I was struggling to overcome pressure. I started singing it as I'd have her on my hip, getting things done, and it gave me peace and joy. May it change pressure to peace for you, too!)

(Fast, victorious! Sing ALL CAPS words louder)

It just gets better
It just gets better
Life just gets better
It just gets better
It just gets better
Amen—
Cause Daddy God's so good!
It just gets better

It just gets better
Life just gets better
Dad, You say in Your Covenant Letter
You say
WE WIN!
I'll sing it again...
(repeat as desired!)

Resurrection Rock

(ATOS 6.06)

You are looking for Jesus...He has risen; - Mark 16:6

Jesus loves you
This is true—
He has a dynamite
Life for you!
He's your best Friend,
Your patient Boss;
He died for you
Upon the cross.
Just ask Him right
Into your heart;
That's the way
Blessed life you start.
He will be with you
Everywhere
Guard your life
With loving care.

Today I Am His Choice!

(ATOS 4.43)

His voice *and* speech are exceedingly sweet; yes, he is altogether lovely [the whole of him delights and is precious]. This is my beloved, and this is my friend, O daughters of Jerusalem! – Song 5:16, AMPC

(confidently, in grateful awe)

I'm a Daughter of the Living God
Wise and victorious!
I'm a Daughter of the Living God
Beautiful and glorious!
I rejoice, rejoice, for
Today I hear His Voice!
I rejoice, rejoice, for
Today He is my Choice!
I'm a Daughter of the Living God
Wise and victorious!
I'm a Daughter of the Living God

Beautiful and glorious!
I rejoice, rejoice, for
Today I hear His Voice!
I rejoice, rejoice, for
Today *I am His* Choice!

The LORD of Hosts is With Me

(ATOS 6.74)

Who is [He then] this King of glory? The Lord of hosts, He is the King of glory. Selah [pause, and think of that]! – Psalm 24:10, AMPC
The Lord of hosts is with us; the God of Jacob is our Refuge (our Fortress and High Tower). Selah [pause, and calmly think of that]! – Psalm 46:7

(sing victoriously!)

I'm not any
Of these things—
(For the LORD my God,
The LORD of hosts
Is with me—
Forever and today!)
Not sick
Not broke
Not endangered
For the LORD my God,
The LORD of hosts

Is with me—
Forever and today!
Not mad
Not sad
Not frustrated
For the LORD my God,
The LORD of hosts
Is with me—
Forever and today!
Not distraught
Not confused
Not abandoned
Not abused
For the LORD my God
The LORD of hosts
Is with me—
Forever and today!
For the LORD my God
The LORD of hosts
Is with me—
Forever and today!

O Lord of hosts, blessed (happy, fortunate, to be envied) is the man who trusts in You [leaning and believing on You, committing all and confidently looking to You, and that without fear or misgiving]! – Psalm 84:12, AMPC

Genius in Jesus

(ATOS 8.02)

FOR WHO HAS KNOWN *or* understood the mind (the counsels and purposes) of the Lord so as to guide *and* instruct Him *and* give Him knowledge? But we have the mind of Christ (the Messiah) *and* do hold the thoughts (feelings and purposes) of His heart. – I Cor. 2:16, AMPC

(with joyful amazement and confidence!)
I'm a GENIUS
IN Jesus—
I AM!
I'm a GENIUS
IN Jesus—
I AM!
1 Corinthians 2:16
Says the truth that's mine—
I have
The Mind of Christ—
The Great I AM!
I'm a GENIUS
IN Jesus—

I AM!
I'm a GENIUS
IN Jesus—
I AM!

And shall make Him of quick understanding, and His delight shall be in the reverential and obedient fear of the Lord. And He shall not judge by the sight of His eyes, neither decide by the hearing of His ears; - Isaiah 11:3, AMPC

Jehovah Nissi

(ATOS 7.24)

"And Moses built an altar and named it 'The LORD is my Banner."
-Exodus 17:15

I love You Adonai Ahuvi!*
Great is Your faithfulness and grace to me
You rescued me from my strong enemy
Your blood eternally set me free!
For all these I praise You, Jehovah Nissi**
Jehovah Nissi, Jehovah Nissi!
My dragon-Slayer! You broke all the bonds
You tore down the idols and the witches' wands
You drove out all the demons
That had made me their pawn
You seared them with Light—
Now they are gone!
For all these I praise You, Jehovah Nissi
Jehovah Nissi, Jehovah Nissi!
For all these I praise You, Jehovah Nissi,
I praise You Jehovah Nissi!
You noticed all my sighing, my weeping and my groans
You breathed Resurrection a to every bone

You raised me to sit beside You on Your throne
Now I'm on altar to Heaven my home!
For all these I praise You Jehovah Nissi
Jehovah Nissi, Jehovah Nissi!
Jehovah Nissi, You are my victory
You raised up Your banner of Love over me
You destroyed the destroyer
And You set me free—
Oh how I praise You
Adonai Ahuvi!*

*Hebrew name for "LORD, My Beloved" and pronounced (approximately—"Ah doe NIGH Ah hoo VEE)

** Hebrew name for "The LORD is my Banner, the LORD is my Miracle." Jehovah Nee SEE

Your Word is Lightnin'

(ATOS 7.91)

...My words will not perish or pass away.—Mark 13:31, AMP
His appearance was like lightning... - Matthew 28:3, AMPC

(Slowly, thoughtfully; deeply joyful, with awe; increasing in strength, speed, and volume)

Your Word is lightnin' to my spirit;
Your Word is lightnin' to my soul!
And I thrill each time I hear it,
'cause greater freedom is your goal!
Your Word is lightnin' to my spirit;
Your Word is lightnin' to my soul!
And I thrill each time I hear it,
'cause greater freedom is your goal—
Your worthy, worthy, worthy goal!
Your worthy, worthy, worthy goal!
YOUR WORTHY WORTHY WORTHY GOAL!

For just as the lightning flashes from the east and shines and is seen as far as the west, so will the coming of the Son of Man be. -
Matthew 24:27, AMPC

The Defeated Devil Blues!

©2016 by Tonja K. Taylor[1]
(ATOS 6.41)

"To the Chief Musician. A Psalm of David. A Song. Let God arise, and His enemies be scattered; Let those who hate Him flee before Him." – Psalm 68:1, AMP

THE LORD GAVE ME THIS in 2016. I laughed, as He revealed this song to me—from the perspective of how the defeated enemy must feel—because Jesus completely stripped and whipped and crushed him at the cross over 2,000 years ago!

So, here's the song, (from the perspective of the whiny, defeated, downcast one—the devil! Sing it soulfully, sorrowfully, in a low voice as the defeated devil speaking.)

Oh, woe, woe—
oh woe is me
I'm whipped for all eternity!
I got the devil's
I got the devil's

1. http://www.faithwriters.com/member-profile.php?id=64826

I got the devil's
broken blues!
I'm so low
that I could die—
instead I'll fry
('cause I did lie)
I got the devil's
I got the devil's
I got the devil's
broken blues!
That Jesus,
He done whipped me—
tripped and flipped and cripped me;
He's made a huge Family
That hate me so much—
whewie!
I tried to accuse 'em
I tried to abuse ‘em
Did my best to use 'em—
But they got wise to me
Realized they are free
With His blood of Victory!
I got the devil's
I got the devil's
I got the devil's
broken blues!
Daily, I lie
try to make 'em cry
But they just look
To His ancient Book
I try to fool 'em
Try to re-school 'em

Say it's lame; that
They'll always be the same
But then—
to my chagrin
They use His Name
They know they win!
Oh woe, woe, woe!
I got the devil's
I got the devil's
I got the devil's
broken blues!
What a crime!
They say I'm slime
curse me all the time—
Take back every dime
That I've stolen—
Seven-fold
(Yeah, He told 'em;
It's gettin' old!)
I got the devil's
I got the devil's
I got the devil's
broken blues!
I have less to take
'cause they're coming awake
And a racket they make
What a blasted headache
As they praise the True
Say I'm under their shoes!
That I owe them dues
What ruse can I use?
Oh what can I do?

My traps they refuse
For my head Jesus bruised
And they say I'm through
Oh woe, woe, woe!
I got the devil's
I got the devil's
I got the devil's
broken blues!
They say it's their earth,
Jeer me with their mirth
Blab about the new birth
I'm in a dearth—oh woe!
Now even though I try
to tell them they'll die
They tell me to fly
And then I do cry
Oh woe, woe, woe!
I got the devil's
I got the devil's
I got the devil's
broken blues!

The reason the Son of God appeared was to destroy the devil's work. - I John 3:8, AMPC

Chrysalis

(ATOS 8.39)

From the womb to the tomb—
From hell to earth
To Heaven Christ did zoom!
Chrysalis; we must make room
The Chrysalis—the transformation
The process of the reformation
Of the dead into the living
Jesus Christ—the Life Who's giving
He came disguised as sinful flesh
Entered humanity's dark mess
To give us life true new and fresh
He is our LORD Atah Kodesh
From the womb to the tomb—
From hell to earth
Then to Heaven Christ did zoom!
Chrysalis; we must make room
On our darkness He will boom
No living life in a vacuum
Nobody should assume
Eternal life till they cocoon
He shattered darkness with His Light

With His unconquerable might
Gave satan Lightmares in the night
and gives us Children right delight
From the womb to the tomb—
From hell to earth
Then to Heaven Christ did zoom!
Chrysalis; we must make room
To restore all that was lost
He paid the ultimate of costs
The devil thought he's won the toss
But that rat God double-crossed!
So then the Renaissance occurred;
Christ rose again—the Living Word;
Now we preach till all have heard
And seeking souls have learned
Because of Jesus' resurrection
We're His objects of affection
He is our Divine Direction
We heed His Royal Voice inflection
From the womb to the tomb—
From hell to earth
Then to Heaven Christ did zoom!
Chrysalis; we must make room!

But he said to them, "Do not be alarmed. You are looking for Jesus the Nazarene, who was crucified. He has risen! He is not here! - Mark 16:6, Berean Standard Bible

...5 For even if there are so-called gods, whether in heaven or on earth (as there are many so-called gods and lords), 6 <u>yet for us there is but one God, the Father, from whom all things came and for whom we exist. And there is but one Lord, Jesus Christ, through whom all things came</u>

and through whom we exist. – I Cor. 8:6, Berean Standard Bible (underline emphasis mine)

The Way Home

©1996 by Tonja K. Taylor[1]
(ATOS 7.54)

Jesus saith unto him, I am the way, the truth, and the life: no man cometh unto the Father, but by me. —John 14:6, KJV

Once I was lost, in place unknown,
was searching for the right way Home.
I saw an old, forgotten book,
and picked it up to have a look
at pages weathered. History
unfolded; this great mystery
revealed to me the power of
the LORD Almighty—God above.
I sat there in His flowered field
from man nor beast nor bird concealed,
and reveled in His wondrous Word.
(How many times before I'd heard
these very phrases told to me
by Believer, by Pharisee)
I clutched the Treasure to my breast
and knew my soul was truly blessed;
lost for so long, that joyful day,
I'd found the right way Home—God's Way!

1. http://www.faithwriters.com/member-profile.php?id=64826

The Son Won!

(ATOS 10.12)

15...THAT EVERYONE WHO believes in Him may have eternal life. 16 For God so loved the world that He gave His one and only Son, that everyone who believes in Him shall not perish but have eternal life. 17 For God did not send His Son into the world to condemn the world, but to save the world through Him... John 3:15-17, Berean Standard Bible

13 Christ redeemed us from the curse of the Law, having become a curse for us—for it is written, "CURSED IS EVERYONE WHO HANGS ON A TREE"— 14 in order that in Christ Jesus the blessing of Abraham might come to the Gentiles, so that we would receive the promise of the Spirit through faith. – Galatians 3:13-14, Berean Standard Bible

It must have rained that Friday on the hill
When leagues of angels wept ten billion tears;
When Love hung as a brother to the thieves
Where Innocence was spoiled and scourged with sin
Nails were not what held Christ to the cross,
But faithful love and grace He fully gave
As He, with outstretched arms embraced the world
And paid our debt forever with His blood.
He could have caused those leagues of angels down

To save Him and destroy this evil world
But Jesus kept His Father's will for us
And conquered hell and death forever more
Sin died that day; the temple veil was rent
Allowing us the precious chance to walk
Across the holy bridge of Jesus Christ
and come through Him into majestic Grace
Oh how the sun did shine upon the hill
That glorious blessed Resurrection Day;
Our LORD and Savior Jesus did arise—
Eternal life to all who come and call!

13 When you were dead in your transgressions and the uncircumcision of your flesh, He made you alive together with Him, having forgiven us all our transgressions, 14 having canceled out the certificate of debt consisting of decrees against us, which was hostile to us; and He has taken it out of the way, having nailed it to the cross. – Colossians 2:13-14, Berean Standard Bible

The Throne

©1992 by Tonja K. Taylor[1]
(ATOS 5.92)

He was always there, rocking;
proudly from his favorite chair
he'd wave to me, forever
content just to see
his small, simple world
from the well-worn boards
he rested on. And each
time he'd smile
his toothless grin,
I'd be filled
with a strange sense of peace.
One glorious day
the chair was empty. Funny
how it looked like just
an old rickety thing
now that its king was gone;
It had seemed
such a cozy throne
when he so happily rocked there.
I knew then he had found
a better place; a silver cloud

1. http://www.faithwriters.com/member-profile.php?id=64826

in the sky. A smile
came, again, as I thought
of him waving,
greeting angels
as they passed by.

For this reason, they are before the throne of God and serve Him day and night in His temple; and the One seated on the throne will spread His tabernacle over them. - Revelation 7:15, Berean Standard Bible

Jesus Reigns In My Everything
Jesús Reina en mi Todo

(ATOS 4.16)

My God reigns!
¡Mi Dios reina!
My God reigns!
¡Mi Dios reina!
My God reigns!
¡Mi Dios reina!
In my everything!
¡En mi todo!
Cause JESUS reigns in my body!
¡Porque JESÚS reina en mi cuerpo!
JESUS reigns in my soul!
¡ JESÚS reina en mi alma!
JESUS reigns in my spirit!
JESÚS reina en mi ***espíritu!***
His blood has made me whole!
Su sangre me ha sanado!

**1 The LORD reigns! He is robed is majesty; the LORD has
clothed and armed Himself with strength. The world indeed is
firmly established; it cannot be moved. 2Your throne was**

established long ago; You are from all eternity.... Psalm 93:1-2, Berean Standard Bible

I Am Free and Very Rich!
Yo Soy Libre y Muy Rico!

(ATOS 3.80)
(sing joyfully and thankfully)
I am free and very rich
Yo soy libre y muy rico
I am free and very rich
Yo soy libre y muy rico
I am free and very rich—
Yo soy libre y muy rico
In Jesus Christ the LORD!
¡en Jesucristo el SEÑOR!
I am free and very rich
Yo soy libre y muy rico
I am free and very rich
Yo soy libre y muy rico
I am free and very rich—
Yo soy libre y muy rico
In Jesus Christ the LORD!
¡en Jesucristo el SEÑOR!

I am free and very rich
Yo soy libre y muy rico

I am free and very rich
Yo soy libre y muy rico
I am free and very rich—
Yo soy libre y muy rico
To the glory of the LORD!
Para la gloria del SENOR!
In Jesus Christ the LORD!
¡en Jesucristo el SEÑOR!
To the glory of the LORD!
Para la gloria del SENOR!

Then you will know the truth, and the truth will set you free.–
Romans 8:31, Berean Standard Bible

The blessing of the LORD enriches, and He adds no sorrow to it. –
Prov. 10:22, Berean Standard Bible

Fantastic Aspirations

(ATOS 9.0)

To catch a bit of moonbeam in a glass
To feel a rainbow's touch upon my skin
To taste the wind and know its secret hues
To rearrange the constellations and to put them back again
To ride a falling star to its destiny
To etch the splendor of a sunset upon my memory
To hear the romance of the music of the Northern Lights
To understand the language of the sea
These are fantastic aspirations; dreamer's dreams;
But possible to the soul that has no seams.

Now to Him who is able to do far more abundantly beyond all that we ask or think, according to the power that works within us, to Him *be* the glory in the church and in Christ Jesus to all generations forever and ever. Amen. – Eph. 3:20-21, Berean Standard Bible

Appearance of a Rainbow

(ATOS 12.0)

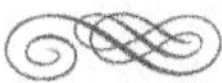

16 When the bow [rainbow] is in the clouds and I look upon it, I will [earnestly] remember the everlasting covenant or pledge between God and every living creature of all flesh that is upon the earth. 17 And God said to Noah, This [rainbow] is the token or sign of the covenant or solemn pledge which I have established between Me and all flesh upon the earth.—Genesis 9:16-17, AMPC

Dove-clouds encircle
the gentle glissades
or harmonious hues
Birds happy with song
sing soft serenades
to angel's bright pews
Heavenly artist
paints on eager eyes
magnificent sight
Dazzling arch enshrines
illumines the skies
with ethereal light
Rapturous image

brings warm accolade
glimpse of holiest Grace
Rainbow-ribbon ties
the Promise God made
with resplendent lace.

Jesus' Christmas Tree

Art by Victoria

ATOS 10.0

If Jesus had a Christmas tree,
Each limb would touch eternity--
branches full of decoration
For each tribe and race and nation;
The names of each engraved upon
An ornament; cherished and known
And crafted into each, and hidden,
Specifics of His missing children;
Each one of their faces
In the farthest of places
Touched by our prayers,
They'll want Jesus there.
His tree is lush and full and tall,
Living, big enough for all
And everywhere, the graceful light
And shepherd's staffs, red and white;

Upon the top, a shining star,
Of Israel, jewel of God's heart;
The symbol with six pointed sides,
Where the King will soon abide;
Streaming from the star above
Cascades of ribbon, crimson love.
Precisely perched, the tiny doves
Seem to sing of those He loves
God loves His children, every one;
To rescue them, He sent His Son
He sent LORD Jesus to redeem
His children, to restore their dream;

For on that ancient Christmas tree--
The tree for all humanity--
He reached throughout eternity
To return them to His family;
It's up to you and up to me
To help Him with His Christmas tree.

We're Harvesting Every Day!

© June 2025 by Tonja K. Taylor
(ATOS 6.43)

The one who sows to please his flesh, from the flesh will reap destruction; but the one who sows to please the Spirit, from the Spirit will reap eternal life. Let us not grow weary in well-doing, for in due time we will reap a heb if we do not give up. – Galatians 6:8-9, Berean Standard Bible (underline mine)

We're harvesting every day
We're harvesting every way
Off every good seed
And every good deed—
We're harvesting every day
YAY YAY!
We're harvesting from the years
Of the good seeds we have sown
We're enjoying the fruitfulness
Of what we planted; my, how it's grown!
Our God is so faithful
To teach us to give; to know
How to increase His worthy Kingdom—
How to help it expand and grow
With our words and our money and our service—

So many people to Him will go!
We're harvesting every day
We're harvesting every way
Off every good seed
And every good deed—
We're harvesting every day
YAY YAY!

Carve Your Marble!

(ATOS 7.48)

This nameless poem has inspired me for over 30 years, and now I share it with you:

(I have self-titled it "Carve Your Marble!")

To each one is given a marble to carve for the wall
A stone that is needed to heighten the beauty of all;
And only your soul has the 'magic' to give it grace,
And only our hands the cunning to put it in place.
Yes, the task that is given to each, no other can do
So the errand is waiting; it has waited through ages for you.
And now you appear, and the hushed ones are turning their gaze
To see what you do with your chance in the chamber of days.
—Edith Hyman, quoted in *The Promotable Woman ©1997*

For the kingdom of God consists of and is based on not talk but power (moral power and excellence of soul). — I Corinthians 4:20 (AMPC)

Princess, the P.O.W.E.R. to change things is in your hand.

What will you do with your P.O.W.E.R.—this hour?

FOR ADDITIONAL INSPIRING spirit songs, poems, humor, and more, check out Tonja's writings on FaithWriters.com, at https://www.faithwriters.com/member-profile.php?id=64826. Also listen to Tonja's edifying "RainWater" podcasts from a few years ago, for a fresh drink of the Spirit's Living Water. A portion of the income (after the tithe) from POWERLight Learning books and other works goes to support organizations that promote the Good News of Jesus Christ, our LORD the King!

"...grace and peace to you from Him who is and was and is to come, and from the seven Spirits before His throne, 5 and from Jesus Christ, the faithful witness, the firstborn from the dead, and the kings of the earth. To Him who loves us and has released us from our sins by His blood. has made us to be a kingdom, priests to His God and Father—to Him be the glory and power forever and ever! Amen...." - Revelation 1:4-6, Berean Standard Bible

They will make war against the Lamb, and the Lamb will triumph over them, because He is Lord of lords and King of kings; and He will be accompanied by His called and chosen and faithful ones."—Revelation 17:14, Berean Standard Bible

Bonus: I Wanna be a Princess

(ATOS 5.09)

(This is part of the prequel; Princess Pearl's history a couple years before *The Adventures of Princess Pearl, P.O.W.E.R. (Purposeful Operations With Eternal Rewards) Girl!* Book I.)

"Mother," announced ten-year-old Pearl one day, "I wanna be a princess."

Her eyes shone as she stood up straighter and said, "I want to wear a royal gown and a royal robe, with rainbows full of sparkles and waterfalls of glittering gold, and a royal crown full of beautiful jewels. I want to sleep in a big, high royal bed with lots of soft mattresses—you know, like in the story. And I want to have a little royal pooch—with a royal 'tude, but sweet too."

"I want to ride a royal horse, white and tall and splendid," she said, dancing around on her tippy-toes. "I want to go on royal adventures to the beach and the mountains and the forest and the mall and by car and train and plane and bicycle, and treat my friends to royal feasts, and say, 'Won't you please come to tea?'"

Her mother nodded, so Pearl continued.

"And Mother, please," she said, speaking more slowly to sound more royal. "I want my own wing of the palace. A Princess needs her privacy, you know."

"Oh, really?" said her mother, and chuckled a bit. "Is that all?"

"That's all. For now," said Pearl.

Her mother smiled and bent down to look into her daughter's earnest eyes. "Ah, my sweet Pearl, I see. It is time for you to meet The King."

"Meet The King?" Pearl said. *This is a little scary, but a lot exciting,* she thought. *There must be more to this princess thing than I thought.*

"Yes. He is a good king," her mother said. "He is the best king. You must meet him and learn his ways, for it's the only way to be a true *Princess of P.O.W.E.R.!"*

Pearl paused. "P.O.W.E.R.?" she said. Excitement rose in her. "When can I start?"

"Right now," said her mother, as she walked to the desk. "Your dad and I will teach you. The first step is to look into The Royal Book; the Holy Bible. It will show you how to be the best kind of Princess there is—and that is a *Princess of Purposeful Operations With Eternal Rewards!"*

For the kingdom of God consists of and is based on not talk but power (moral power and excellence of soul). — I Corinthians 4:20 (AMPC)

(Books I-V of The Adventures of Princess Pearl, P.O.W.E.R. Girl! will be available in ebook and paperback, early this summer! Books VI-VIII are in process. Check them out, and thank you for your prayers!)

Index

Don't miss out!

Visit the website below and you can sign up to receive emails whenever Tonja K. Taylor publishes a new book. There's no charge and no obligation.

https://books2read.com/r/B-A-HSCAB-XXIJG

BOOKS 2 READ

Connecting independent readers to independent writers.

Did you love *P.O.W.E.R. Princess Poetry Plus*? Then you should read *The Adventures of Princess Pearl, P.O.W.E.R. Girl!*[1] by Tonja K. Taylor!

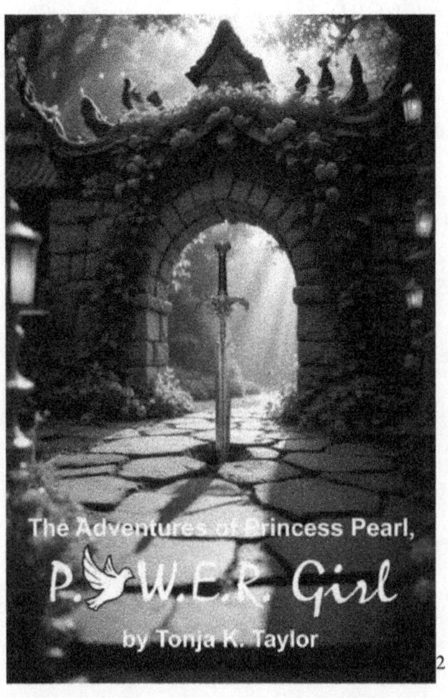
The Adventures of Princess Pearl,
P. W.E.R. Girl
by Tonja K. Taylor
[2]

After her dear dad is killed in a motorcycle accident, Princess Pearl moves with her mother and little brother Robert to the mountains of northwest Arkansas, to live with their Uncle Burt on his beautiful 200-acre ranch. There, the LORD works healing in their hearts. They make new Latino friends, start attending Burt's church, and continue with homeschool. Also, they get new horses--including a super-special surprise for Pearl--and have lots of interesting adventures. God even helps Pearl start learning to be nicer to her little brother, Robert. Most of all, she learns to trust her Daddy God more—for the small things, and the huge ones.

---

1. https://books2read.com/u/bzwEgz

2. https://books2read.com/u/bzwEgz

Read more at https://www.faithwriters.com/member-profile.php?id=64826.

Also by Tonja K. Taylor

POWERLight Lit Tips for Better Teaching
The New Legacy Expanded
P.O.W.E.R. Princess Poetry Plus
The Adventures of Princess Pearl, P.O.W.E.R. Girl!
Your Holy Health: Effective Secrets to Divine Life
Spirit Songs & Stories Enhanced

Watch for more at https://www.faithwriters.com/member-profile.php?id=64826.

About the Author

From her adventure series, THE ADVENTURES OF PRINCESS PEARL, P.O.W.E.R. (Purposeful Operations With Eternal Rewards) Girl!; to her many other books; to her YouTube channel, "River Rain Creative"; to her service at church; to her presentations in schools, community, and online across the globe, Tonja and her husband delight to help others to see the LORD Jesus Christ, our soon-returning Savior and King!

Read more at https://www.faithwriters.com/member-profile.php?id=64826.

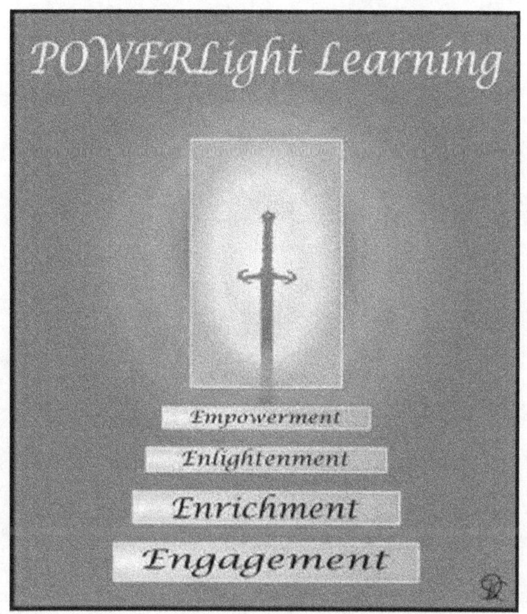

About the Publisher

Through engagement and enrichment comes enlightenment and empowerment—for bad or for good.

The book publishing arm of POWERLight Learning is based on Romans 5:19 and 12:2, and engages, enriches, enlightens, and empowers readers through positively provocative works for good, for God; *"Because what you read matters!"*

As the eternal, infallible, unchanging Word of God states: "***For the kingdom of God consists of and is based on not talk but power (moral power and excellence of soul).***" - I Corinthians 4:20, AMPC

It is our prayer that works by POWERLight Learning will draw all who experience them to a deeper love and loyalty to the LORD Jesus Christ, our soon-returning King!

Read more at https://www.faithwriters.com/member-profile.php?id=64826.

www.ingramcontent.com/pod-product-compliance
Lightning Source LLC
Chambersburg PA
CBHW021200020426
42331CB00003B/138

* 9 7 8 1 9 6 5 6 4 1 2 4 8 *